Written by Heather Dakota
Illustrated by Nancy Panaccione & Dan Jankowski
Designed by Nancy Panaccione

Tangerine Press
an imprint of
SCHOLASTIC
www.scholastic.com

Scholastic and Tangerine Press and associated logos are trademarks of Scholastic Inc.

Published by Tangerine Press, an imprint of Scholastic Inc., 557 Broadway, New York, NY 10012

10 9 8 7 6 5 4 3 2 1
ISBN: 978-0-545-70082-5

Printed and bound in Guangzhou, China

Photo Credits:
iStockphoto: Man looking into volcano: box and cover, top left, p5 bottom (Yulkapopkova); Hand holding rock: box and cover, top center, p3 inset, p22 top inset, (mercedes rancaño); Lava flow: box and cover, top right (trait2lumiere), p4 (filipewiens), p25, inset, bottom (matteo69), p28, inset (StephanHoerold); White lava rock: box and cover (Oktay Ortakcioglu); Volcanic eruptions: box and cover, p8: (Beboy ltd), p16 (AZ68), p20, inset bottom, p30 and 31, insets (AZ68); p5, inset top (mikeuk); p9, background (PaulCowan); p10, background (vicnt); Beaker: p12 (claylib); p21, inset, top (LindaMarieB), p21, bottom right (Musimon); p22, bottom (memoangeles); p24, inset, bottom (NickolayV), p20, inset, top (romkaz); p27, arrowhead (trekandshoot), arrow, right: (Denny Thurston), Media Bakery: p11, top (Jose Luis Stephens); Minden Pictures: p11, bottom (Pete Oxford); Science Source: p10, inset (Bill Bachmann/Photo Researchers). Wegraphics.net : Backgrounds: 1, 2; 6, 20, 22, 23; paper: 3, 12, 13.

TABLE OF CONTENTS

Welcome
All You Rock Stars!

ROCKS ARE SOME OF THE MOST INTERESTING AND IMPORTANT THINGS ON EARTH.

Don't believe it?

From the ground you walk on to the sand at the bottom of the ocean, rocks are the basic building blocks of the earth.

The rocks in your kit are all unpolished igneous rocks. That means at one time they were inside a volcano.

Turn the page to discover the hot world of volcanoes and the igneous rocks that they produce.

WHERE DO IGNEOUS ROCKS COME FROM?

When the lava cools igneous rocks are formed.

VOLCANIC ROCK EXPERTS

If you love volcanoes, check out these careers where you can be around volcanoes and volcanic rocks all the time.

Volcanologists study one of the earth's most explosive processes—volcanoes! Most volcanologists have college degrees in geology, chemistry, physics, computer science, or math.

And these jobs are dangerous, too!

Physical volcanologists study how and why volcanoes erupt as well as deposits from volcanic eruptions.

Geophysicists study earthquakes and how they relate to volcanoes and other properties of the earth, like gravity.

Geochemists study the products of volcanoes to understand what chemicals make up rocks, gas, and lava.

IGNEOUS ROCKS ARE CALLED "FIRE ROCKS."

They can form underground or above ground. When melted rock, called magma, deep inside the earth becomes trapped in small pockets and begins to cool, igneous rock is formed. It can also form when volcanoes erupt, causing magma to rise above the Earth's surface, becoming lava.

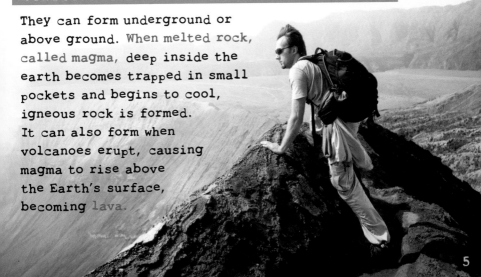

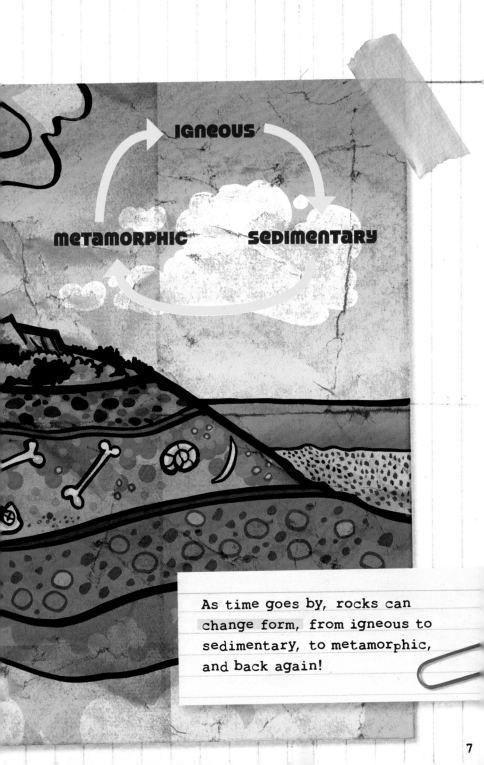

IGNEOUS

METAMORPHIC SEDIMENTARY

As time goes by, rocks can change form, from igneous to sedimentary, to metamorphic, and back again!

IGNEOUS ROCKS

THE WORD IGNEOUS COMES FROM A GREEK WORD MEANING "OF FIRE."

Igneous (pronounced IG-nee-us) Rocks

are the oldest type of rocks. Igneous refers to one of the three major types of rocks. Metamorphic and sedimentary are the other two. Igneous rock is formed when magma cools and solidifies, either above or below the Earth's surface. Deep inside the Earth, the temperature is very high and the minerals are in a liquid form called magma. As the magma pushes to the Earth's surface, it starts to cool and turn into solid igneous rock.

There are **MORE THAN 700** different types of igneous rocks, including the rocks in your kit.

What's the Difference?

INTRUSIVE vs EXTRUSIVE IGNEOUS ROCKS

All igneous rocks do not cool the same way. That is why they do not look all the same.

INTRUSIVE ROCK

Some cool slowly, deep under the Earth's surface. This is called an intrusive igneous rock. It is easy to identify these rocks because magma cools very slowly under the Earth's surface, allowing crystals to grow big enough to view with the naked eye. Some intrusive rocks are granite, diorite, rhyolite, and gabbro.

RHYOLITE

BASALT

OBSIDIAN

PUMICE

EXTRUSIVE ROCK

Other rocks formed when magma erupts from a volcano or reaches the earth's surface through long cracks. Lava cools quickly and forms rocks with small crystals. These are called extrusive igneous rocks. Basalt, obsidian, and pumice are examples of this type of igneous rock.

Cooling speed determines rock type.

VOLCANOES 101

Volcanoes have awesome fiery natures that have left whole cities destroyed and killed tens of thousands of people. They are formed when magma deep within the Earth works its way to the surface and erupts to form lava and ash deposits.

TYPES OF VOLCANOES

CINDER CONE VOLCANOES

(also called scoria cones) are the most common type of volcano. They have a symmetrical cone shape. The lava cools super-fast and builds up around the vent, forming a crater. Cinder cone volcanoes are usually small, about 300 ft. (91 m) tall. Dragon Cone in British Columbia, Canada is a cinder cone volcano.

AIRBORNE FRAGMENTS OF LAVA, CALLED TEPHRA, ARE EJECTED FROM A SINGLE VENT.

VEI= Volcanic Explosivity Index

MAGMA VS LAVA
MAGMA IS CALLED LAVA
when it reaches the Earth's surface.

STRATOVOLCANOES
are also called composite
volcanoes because they are
built from many layers of
lava flow, ash, and blocks
of unmelted stone. They
are larger rising up to
8,000 feet, (2,438 meters).
Stratovolcanoes have a
system of vents leading
from a magma pool deep
below the earth's surface.
Stratovolcanoes can erupt

with great violence, not only from the top but from the
sides, too. Magma and gas builds up over time. When it
is released, gases explode, like soda shooting out of a
soda can. Mount St. Helens is a stratovolcano.

SHIELD VOLCANOES are giant, gently sloping
volcanoes made from very thin lava spreading out in
all directions from a central vent. They have wide
bases with steep middle slopes and a flatter summit.
Eruptions are not usually explosive, more like liquid
overflowing the edges of a container. Mauna Loa in
Hawaii, is a shield volcano.

Experiment 1:

ADULT HELPER NEEDED

MAKE A VOLCANO

You're probably not going to see a real volcano in your backyard. So, what could be better than making one that oozes all over the place and no one gets hurt?

YOU'LL NEED:

- ○ Newspaper
- ○ 3 heaping teaspoons (13 g) Baking soda
- ○ Dish detergent
- ○ Red food coloring
- ○ Beaker or narrow glass
- ○ Pie tin or baking sheet (something to catch the lava)
- ○ 2 cups (.5 L) White vinegar

Let's get messy!

WHAT YOU'LL DO:

BE CAREFUL!
Food coloring can stain!

1 Lay newspapers on your work surface and get a parent to help you.

2 Add a few drops of food coloring into the vinegar to create the lava color. Shake it well to mix in the color.

3 Place the beaker on the baking sheet. Add the baking soda into the empty beaker.

4 Add a couple of drops of dish detergent into the beaker.

5 When you're ready, pour the colored vinegar into the beaker.

6 Watch the lava flow!

7 Don't forget to clean up.

RING OF FIRE

The **RED** areas are volcanoes.

TOP 10 DEADLIEST
VOLCANIC ERUPTIONS IN HISTORY

10 ### MT. VESUVIUS, 79 AD
Deaths: estimated 3,360 people

When Mt. Vesuvius blew in 79 AD, it left the entire cities of Pompeii and Herculaneum buried under a blanket of ash and pumice (ash flow) that rained down for nearly an entire day. The people didn't have time to escape the volcano's fury. They were buried and preserved just as they were when the volcano erupted.

9 ### MT. VESUVIUS, 1631
Deaths: 3,500 recorded
(possibly as high as 6,000)

On December 16, 1631 between 6:00 and 7:00 AM, Mt. Vesuvius unexpectedly erupted. Darkness fell over the entire area, and earthquakes occurred every 1 to 15 minutes. Just when it couldn't get any worse, rain began to fall, which started a mudflow. Lava flows started soon after that. The continuous earthquakes started a tsunami that hit the shores with waves at heights of 24 to 60 ft. (7.3 to 18.3 m).

8 ### GALUNGGUNG, INDONESIA, 1882
Deaths: 4,011 people

Galunggung is a stratovolcano on the island of Java. In October of 1882, Mt. Galunggung erupted. This eruption blanketed all the surrounding areas with ash and mudflow.

7 ### KELUT, INDONESIA, 1919
Deaths: 5,110 people

On the island of Java in May of 1919, mudflows and lakes of lava flowed fast into nearby settlements. It dusted villages up to 8 mi. (13 km) away with ash.

6 ### LAKI, ICELAND, 1783
Deaths: 9,350 people due to famine

Laki is a legendary Icelandic volcano, which has been dormant since its huge eruption in 1783. The clouds of poisonous gases killed more than 50 percent of the livestock population and resulted in a famine. The after-effects of this eruption were felt all over the world. The winter of 1784 was the longest and one of the coldest on record.

5 UNZEN, JAPAN, 1792

Deaths: 14,300 people

The 4,921 ft. (1,500 m) volcano, which is still active, had its most noteworthy eruption in 1792. A recent eruption in 1991 killed 43 people, including three notable volcanologists.

4 NEVADA DEL RUIZ, COLOMBIA, 1985

Deaths: 25,000 people

Nevado Del Ruiz is located in Colombia. It is also known for its deadly lahars, a type of boiling mudflow. The village of Armero was built on top of the dried magma. In 1985, the town was completely buried under a boiling mudflow moving at 40 mph (64.5 kph).

3 MT. PELÉE, MARTINIQUE, 1902

Deaths: 29,025 people

Mount Pelée is on the Caribbean island of Martinique. During the 1902 eruption, residents watched for several days as the volcano shot steam and gas into the air. On May 8, Mount Pelée erupted violently. The ground shook, and gas, ash, and rock barreled into St. Pierre at more than 100 mph (161 kph). Witnesses on ships said there was a sudden mushroom cloud, which consumed the island in seconds.

2 KRAKATOA, INDONESIA, 1883

Deaths: 36,417 people

The island of Krakatoa is between the islands of Java and Sumatra. When Krakatoa blew its top in 1883, it did so with the force of 200 megatons of TNT. The eruption destroyed almost the entire island, and was heard all the way in Australia (2,294 miles, 3,692 km away).

1 TAMBORA, INDONESIA, 1815

Deaths: more than 92,000 people due to lava flows and toxic fumes, many more worldwide due to starvation

The most deadly and devastating volcanic eruption was on the island of Sumbawa. Entire villages were buried under lava flows. Ten thousand people were killed almost instantly. So much ash was thrown into the atmosphere when Tambora exploded that it blocked out sunlight and solar radiation, causing a 37.5 °F (3 °C) temperature difference. Thus, 1816 became known as the Year Without a Summer.

and eat!

MAKE AN IGNEOUS ROCK

Making a real igneous rock would be hot work.
Wouldn't it be more fun to eat an igneous rock?

Oh yeah!

MATERIALS NEEDED:

○ White chocolate chips
○ Red Food Coloring

white chocolate CHIPS

CREATE AN IGNEOUS ROCK:

1 Ask an adult to help you melt the white chocolate and a few drops of red dye on the stove.

2 When the white chocolate is heated, it's just like magma or melted rocks.

3 Then have an adult help you take spoonfuls of the melted chocolate and plop it onto waxed paper.

4 Let them cool for a few hours.

5 Now you have edible igneous rocks.

Hot rocks! Good eats!

TRIVIA AND FUN FACTS

PLATO

Plato was not only a philosopher but also an early volcanologist.

The earliest known recording of a volcanic eruption is a wall painting dated to about 7,000 BCE in modern-day Turkey.

The upper section of the Earth's crust is made up of around 95% igneous rock.

Kelauea means "spewing" in Hawaiian. Mt. Kilauea in Hawaii may not be the most explosive, violent or destructive volcano, but it's been constantly erupting for more than 20 years. It is one of the world's most active volcanoes.

A layer of igneous rock was discovered in Southwest China. They believe that a huge volcanic eruption that happened 260 million years ago may have killed off many species around the world.

It is believed that the fury of the Santorini eruption of 1645 BC may have led to stories of the lost city of Atlantis.

In the Philippines, the eruption of Mount Pinatubo in 1991 threw 20 million tons of sulfur dioxide into the air. This caused a global cooling that dropped worldwide temperatures.

An underwater volcanic eruption took place 93 million years ago and killed many of the ocean's species.

There is a super-volcano located under Yellowstone National Park. It last erupted 700,000 years ago and may have led to the last Ice Age.

Some granite in Australia is believed to be more than four billion years old.

Earth's moon is made out of igneous rocks.

Igneous rocks contain many minerals that help plants grow.

ROCK COLLECTING 101

Rock collecting is fun and easy.

WHY?

Because rocks are everywhere!
You could collect them for years and years and still have alot more waiting for you to discover.

ROCK COLLECTING is a safe hobby as long as you follow a few guidelines. If you go out rock collecting, always take a buddy. And don't collect around old mines or quarries. NEVER enter tunnels or holes. These are often unstable and could collapse.

Let's get rocking

- Collect and clean specimens.

- Make a label that has the name of the rock and the location where it was collected.

- Assign a number to each rock.

- In a notebook, record the name, location where you found it, and the number of the rock.

- Take a photo to help you identify the rock later.

Find a rock collecting mentor, someone who knows all about rock collecting and can guide you.

DON'T KNOW ANYONE LIKE THAT?

Ask your parents to help you. Or ask at your school, museum, or library. There's bound to be another rockhound who can help get you started.

PINK GRANITE

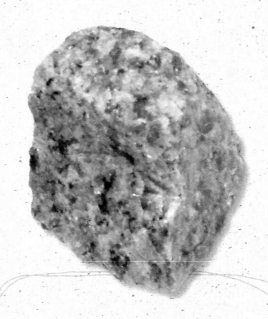

Granite is a common rock that contains at least 25 percent quartz and is sometimes used in construction because of its strength.

Color: light pink

In Ancient Egypt, pink granite was used to build the insides of the Pyramids of Giza.

PERIDOTITE

The peridot gemstone is produced from peridotite rock. It is rarely found on the Earth's surface. It is believed that Earth's mantle is made up of this type of rock. It has an extremely high melting point.

Color: Olive Green

RHYOLITE

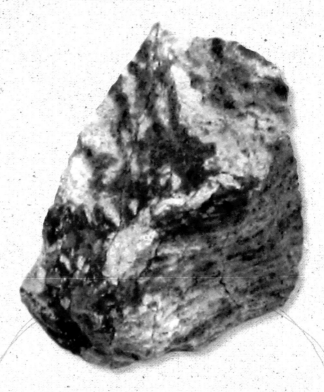

Rhyolite crystals are often too small to see. Actually, it has the same chemistry as granite, but the magma cools very quickly forming rhyolite. If the rhyolite lava doesn't form crystals, it is obsidian.

Color: even or in bands of white, gray, green, red, or brown

Obsidian

Obsidian is a volcanic glass that forms quickly without crystal growth, it can have very sharp edges making it useful as a cutting tool or arrowhead.

Color: black, brown, or green

Obsidian was used in ancient times for making arrowheads, spear points, knife blades, and scrapers.

27

BASALT

Recent studies of Basalt are helping scientists understand how our planet formed billions of years ago. Basalt is formed from cooling lava. It is the most common form of igneous rock.

Color: black

Pumice

Pumice is an unusual, lightweight rock formed when molten rock is rapidly blown out of a volcano, forming bubbles as it quickly loses pressure and cools at the same time.

Color: tan or light gray (more glassy looking than scoria)

Quick Experiment:

Put your pumice is water. Does it float?
A lot of pumice specimens are so light that they float.

SCORIA

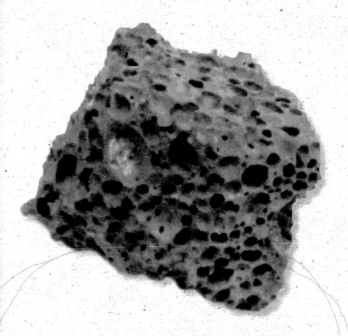

Scoria is blasted out of a volcano.
It is full of bubble holes where lava
cooled around trapped gas.

Color: black, dark gray, reddish brown